D1067395

THE WISDOM OF THE EAST SERIES

EDITED BY J. L. CRANMER-BYNG, M.C.

A FLIGHT OF SWANS

A Flight of Swans

Poems from Balākā

By

RABINDRANATH TAGORE

Translated from the Bengali
by Aurobindo Bose, M.A. (Cantab.)

With a Foreword by
Professor Radhakrishnan, D.Litt, F.B.A.

John Murray, Albemarle Street,
London, W.

First Edition . . . *1955*

88647

Printed in Great Britain by Butler & Tanner Ltd., Frome and London
and Published by John Murray (Publishers) Ltd.

FOREWORD

SRI AUROBINDO BOSE has brought out in his small book a readable English translation of some of Rabindranath Tagore's poems. Tagore's writings, which reveal penetration of mind, magic of poetry and intensity of spirit, give utterance to the dreams and aspirations of humanity. The essential message of India that the Transcendent Supreme is immanent in man and therefore the individual is sacred, is expressed in a variety of ways in Tagore's prose and poetry, song and drama.

Today when the spirit of violence is threatening to desecrate the world of man, when the fumes of hatred are darkening the whole atmosphere, Tagore's teaching, which asks us not to lose faith in the spirit of man, is most timely. He is fond of quoting a great saying of the *Mahābhārata* : " By unrighteousness, man prospers, gains what appears desirable, conquers enemies but perishes at the root." We must give up faith in military power as a solvent for human problems and learn to live nobly and practise love even towards our enemies. It is the only way by which we can build a social structure which will provide enduring peace and human freedom.

S. RADHAKRISHNAN.

The original Bengali Edition
was dedicated by Tagore to
the late W. W. Pearson,
a Quaker and friend of India.

To the Sacred Memory
of GURUDEV
Who lives in our hearts.

CONTENTS

Note on Pronunciation

" ā " means that the vowel is sounded like the " a "
in " father ".

EDITORIAL NOTE

THE object of the Editor of this series is a very definite one. He desires above all things that these books shall be the ambassadors of good-will between East and West. He hopes that they will contribute to a fuller knowledge of the great cultural heritage of the East, for only through real understanding will the West be able to appreciate the underlying problems and aspirations of Asia today. He is confident that a deeper knowledge of the great ideals and lofty philosophy of Eastern thought will help to a revival of that true spirit of charity which neither despises nor fears the nations of another creed and colour.

J. L. CRANMER-BYNG.

50, ALBEMARLE STREET,
LONDON, W.1.

x

TRANSLATOR'S PREFACE

It is with some diffidence that I publish these translations, for I have been a student of science all my life, and made no study of literature at college. However, I had the unique privilege of studying for five years as a boy in the school, *Brahma-Vidyālay*, started by Rabindranath Tagore (whom we called *Gurudev*, the revered *Guru* or Master) at Sāntiniketan,* in the heart of rural Bengal. During these years and later I often heard him recite his poems and explain them to us. Thus, imperceptibly, the seeds of poetry must have grown within me, and now, in the autumn of my life, have come to fruit. A few years ago I could not, even in wildest fancy, have thought it possible for me to undertake this sacred task of translating my revered *Guru* into English verse. But the ways of Providence are strange indeed ; and today, urged by an inner impulse, I had to undertake it.

I have tried my very best to make as literal a translation as possible of the original verses, even at the cost of sounding a little strange to English ears. In this purpose I have been strengthened by the opinions of two great poets—Goethe and Browning. Goethe writes :

There are two great maxims of translation—either turn the foreign author into a native author *or induce the reader to go out to the author's foreignness*. (My italics.)

I have followed the second advice of this great Olympian. And Browning writes of a translation from the Greek :

I should require the translation *to be literal at every cost*, save that of absolute violence to our language. I would be tolerant of even a

---

clumsy attempt to furnish me with the very turn of each phrase in as Greek a fashion as English will bear. (My italics.)

The scent of the Indian *Champak* must not be transmuted into that of an English flower—its charm lies in its very uniqueness. . I have thus purposely kept many Indian words in the English text, and given notes explaining their exact meaning. It no doubt demands more intellectual effort on the part of the reader—but one desiring to come to the classics of Eastern literature should be prepared to make this effort gladly.

Most of the *Balākā* * poems were written during the First World War, and a few before, at Ramgarh in the Himalayas, at Allahabad, Sāntiniketan, and on the banks of the *Padma*. The tiny volume of forty-five poems is a landmark in Bengali literature, both because it introduces new verse forms, and because of the wide sweep of its thought. It is considered to be one of Tagore's masterpieces. In many of these poems there breathes youth's spirit of revolt against the old, who had made a mess of the world—a true reflection of what millions of war-scarred young men felt who returned from the battle-fields of Europe, eager to remake the world nearer to the heart's desire. If that dream failed, it was nevertheless a noble dream—and it is remarkable that Tagore, from the remote corner of a village in the Himalayas, like a sensitive barometer recorded faithfully this *Zeitgeist*. It would be appropriate, I think, if I quote a few passages from letters written to his friends. He writes :

The feelings that were aroused in me when I wrote *Balākā* are still alive within me. They came rushing like a flight of swans, and like them flew from the poet's mind towards the Unknown with an eager restlessness that is inexpressible. . . . Their wings not only disturbed the silence of the twilight, but awakened (in me) the voice of the Infinite—that is the real meaning. . . . Therefore I have named the

---

* It means ' A flock of swans '.

volume *Balākā*. . . .   Perhaps there is an invisible inner link holding the poems together. . . .   The thoughts that became conscious in me were not merely those of war. . . .   Through the war came the call inviting men to a feast of universal brotherhood. . . .   I felt that humanity had arrived at the crossroads—behind us lies the past and the night is coming to an end, while, piercing death and sorrow, the red dawn of a new age is breaking through.   Therefore, for a reason which was not apparent, my mind was so agitated !

He goes on to say that savants like Romain Rolland and Bertrand Russell suffered persecution and unpopularity during the war for holding high ' above the battle ' these ideals of brotherhood and internationalism, and that he had inwardly allied himself with them.

In my mind I had already taken sides.   I had accepted the invitation of one side.   Some people had acknowledged that invitation and some had not.   The first growth of that feeling in me was expressed in *Balākā*.   For some time I had been groping along the hazy path I was invited to follow ; and under the impulse of this feeling, though I did not know it at the time, these poems arose.   They are like so many flags marking the path I was to travel.   What at that time was only a feeling, and found unclear expression in my poems, is today a firm realization, and with it I have arrived at a definite goal.

It was the urge of these same ideals which led him in 1920–1 to make an extensive tour of Europe and America, preaching mutual understanding and reconciliation among all the nations of the earth.   And on his return home, he transformed his tiny poet's school into an international university (*Vishva-Bhārati*).*

The message that he then brought to the West, and which finds lyrical expression in many of the *Balākā* poems, is best given in the poet's own words :

---

* *Vishva* = Universe ; *Bhārati* = Goddess of Learning and Music.   Its motto, in *Sanskrit*, means : ' Where the whole world forms into a nest.'

The God of Humanity has arrived at the gates of the ruined temple of the tribe. Though he has not found his altar, I ask men of simple faith, wherever they may be in the world, to bring their offering of sacrifice to him. I ask them to claim the right of manhood to be friends of men. I ask once again, let us dreamers of the East and West keep our faith in the life that creates and not in the machine that constructs.

With this background, I hope the reader will be better able to understand the *Balākā* poems.*

For the convenience of Bengali readers, I have retained the poem numbers of the Bengali edition, with the exception of the first and thirty-sixth poems, which have been transposed.

In conclusion, it is my pleasant task to express my deep gratitude and thanks to Dr. Radhakrishnan, F.B.A., D.Litt. (Oxon. and Cantab.), Vice-President of India, for his valuable Foreword, which illuminates the background of Indian religious thought, in which Tagore found his deepest spiritual nourishment ; Mrs. Frances Cornford of Cambridge and Mr. Jon Swan of Boston (U.S.A.) for their helpful criticism, and to Dr. B. C. Roy, Chief Minister of West Bengal, for a Government grant.

ÉCOLE D'HUMANITÉ,
 GOLDERN (BERNER OBERLAND),
  SWITZERLAND.
   Easter, 1954.

---

* Those who are interested in the life and work of Tagore should read . *Rabindranath Tagore, Poet and Dramatist*, by J. E. Thompson (London, 1948).

THE meandering current of the Jhelum,
Like a curved sword, glistening in the twilight,
Merges into darkness.
At the ebb of day comes the tide of night
Carrying myriads of star-flowers
Floating on its dark waters.
At the foot of the dark mountains
Stand in rows the *deodar trees*,
As if creation would whisper in dreams,
Unable to utter its message clearly.
Only the gathering of unuttered sounds
Rumbles in the dark.

Suddenly I hear,
In the vast emptiness of the evening sky
The lighting flash of sounds
Shattering from the far to the far beyond.
O flying swans, [1]
Your wings drunk with the wine of tempest
And scattering peals of joyous laughter,
Raise waves of wonder in the still sky.
This music of the wings,
This singing of celestial nymphs,
Fled past,
Disturbing the meditation of silence.
The mountains in their dark slumber shuddered,
The forest of *deodars* shivered,
As if the music of the wings
Brought for an instant the rhythm of movement

Into the heart of joyous immobility.
The mountains yearned
To become the aimless cloud of summer,
The trees to take wing
And follow the trails of sound
And search the ends of space.
O winged wanderer,
Breaking the dreams of twilight
Waves of anguish arise,
Yearning for the beyond.
In the heart of the Universe echoed the burning refrain :
" Not here, not here, somewhere far beyond."

O flying swans,
Tonight you have opened for me the door of silence.
Behind her veil, in earth, sky, water,
I hear the restless beating of wings.
The grass is fluttering its wings in the sky of earth ;
In the brooding darkness of the earth
Who knows what myriads of budding seeds
Are spreading their wings ?
Tonight,
I behold this mountain, this forest,
Spreading their wings,
Winging from island to island,
Soaring from unknown to unknown.
To the beating of the wings of stars
Throbs the cry of light in darkness.

I hear the countless voices of the human heart
Flying unseen,
From the dim past to the dim unblossomed future.
Hear, within my own breast,

The fluttering of the homeless bird which,
In company with countless others,
Flies day and night,
Through light and darkness,
From shore to shore unknown.
The void of the Universe is resounding with the music
of wings :
" Not here, not here, somewhere far beyond."

1. In Bengali the word is *Hansa-balākā*, to pious Hindus a symbol of
the human soul winging its way to its heavenly resting-place.

Now the All-Destroying is come.
The flood cries and heaves
In the sea of pain.
Flashes pierce through the crimson cloud
And thunder roars beyond the forest edge.
What madman is breaking out again and again
In boisterous laughter ?
Now the All-Destroying is come.

Life is now drunk with the sport of death.
Welcome Him now with all the   a have.
Look neither to the right nor
Keep nothing hidden,
And touch His feet with your forehead.
Now the All-Destroying is come.

Make the open road your own.
The room darkens and the flame dies out.
The storm has come and swept through your chamber.
The foundations have tottered.
Do you not hear,
The call has come from the Beyond ?
Now the All-Destroying is come.

Fie ! Shed no tears
Nor cover your face in fear.
What makes your heart tremble ?
Break all your chains
And rush forward towards
What is beyond joy and suffering.

Shall not the paean of victory ring in your voice?
Thy anklets keep time with the dance of *Rudra*? [2]
This play is your destiny—
Casting away all,
Come in your bridal dress of crimson.
Now the All-Destroying is come.

1. This poem reads like a prophecy of the First World War, that was shortly to break out.
2. Another name for Lord Shiva, which means, The Terrible One.

WE march forward,
Who shall stop us?
Those who remain behind
Cry, they shall cry,
With bleeding feet
Shall we mount our obstacles,
And run forward
In shadow and sun.
But they shall get caught
In their own noose,
And cry, they shall cry.

The Terrible One has called us
Blowing his trumpet,
And over our heads resounds
The call of the midday sun.
My mind spreads through the sky,
And I am drunk
With the fountain of light.
But they sit, barring their doors;
Their eyes shall be dazed,
And cry, they shall cry.

The mountains and sea
Shall I conquer.
The lonely path frightens me not,
For He is with me.
But they are giddy,
Whirling round their narrow circles

And frightened to cross the threshold.
For cry, they call cry.

Shiva, the Terrible One, shall arise
Blowing his trumpet
And all bondage burn to ashes.
His ensign shall flutter in the wind
And all doubts vanish.
Churning the sea of death
Shall I seize the elixir of immortality,
While they, clinging to life,
Shall be caught in the coils of death !

YOUR trumpet lies in the dust,
How can I endure it ?
The winds drop
And the lights dim ;
What misfortune threatens us ?
He who would fight,
Let him come with his banner ;
He who has voice,
Let him break into song ;
And he who would march,
Let him run,
Come, O fearless One !
Neglected in the dust your trumpet lies.

I was on the way to the temple
Carrying my offering of flowers
And seeking a haven of peace
At the end of the day.
A hope gleamed in me,
That all wounds would heal
And pure should I emerge,
Washed of all stains.
But on the way I find
Neglected in the dust your trumpet lies.

Shall I light my temple lamps ?
Shall I weave my garland of roses ?
I thought, at the end of my struggles
I should find rest,

And paying off all debts
Find the warmth of your lap.
Then the silent call
Came from your trumpet suddenly.

O touch me with your alchemy.
In luminous song
Let the joy of the radiant heart vibrate.
Piercing the heart of darkness with your awakening call
Spread terror through the four quarters of the world.
With both hands I shall raise today
Your trumpet of victory !

I know, I know,
Sleep will leave me,
Like showers of July.
Some will run to succour me,
Others cry out in fear,
While the bed of sleep will shiver in terror.
For your trumpet today shall
Resound exultantly.

Having sought ease of you
I stand shamed.
Clothe, O clothe me,
In your battle-armour.
Come impediments ever new,
Rain blows ever severe,
Unflinching shall I stand,
And my agony resound
Through your paean of victory !
I shall pour out all strength,
And clasp triumphantly
Your trumpet.

9

On this dark night my boatman has gone crossing the wild seas
The tempest has risen,
Turning his sail to it he goes swiftly.
With fear of the ink-black night the sky shudders and faints ;
The flocks of impatient waves are wild,
And having lost the way are dancing savagely.
In this night of distress,
What troubles the mind of the boatman sailing adrift ?

On such a night, what tryst is this of my boatman ?
With white sails shining in the dark
Comes his boat gliding.
Where will it touch the shore to find her ?
At what hidden threshold burns the lamp of worship ?
Giving her his love, my lonely boatman gives her life.

In this tempest, in this darkness,
What strange search is this of my wandering boatman ?
Perhaps he comes heavy with treasures ?
No, no, neither gems nor gold go with him,
But only a wreath of roses.
Carrying it,
He will cross the dark seas
Singing a careless song.
When the new dawn breaks,
On whose neck will the boatman place this garland ?

She for whom the boatman sailed on this night of distress
Dwells by the wayside.

Unseen he rowed his boat towards her.
Through the ragged walls the wind howls
And the tiny flame trembles lengthening its shadow.
Her name, which you know not,
Is on his lips as he sails.

Many an hour has passed away since the boatman left his shore.
The night has not yet merged into dawn,
Nor is the hour of arrival nigh.
There will be no beating of drums,
Nor anyone knowing he is come ;
Only darkness shall vanish
And light flood the room,
His poverty end
And his body be blessed
By such a thrilled touch.

ART thou a picture, only a picture?
Art thou not as real as the distant stars
Which cluster in the heavens, travelling through the darkness
With lights in their hands?
Art thou not as true as these?
Alas, only a picture, nothing more?

Why dost thou remain still, amidst the ever changing?
Join with the travellers,
O thou that hast missed the way.
Why dost thou keep thyself so far from all,
Hidden in the sanctuary of thy stillness?
The dust that lifts its grey mantle
And sweeps in a whirlwind,
The grass that grows and covers the earth,
They are real because they change and move;
But thou alone art quiet and motionless.
Thou art a picture, only a picture.

Once didst thou move by our side along the road;
The life blood in thy limbs spoke in so many songs and dances,
Throbbing to the pulse of the universe.
In this life, in my world, how real thou wert.
It is thou that has fashioned the soul of Beauty
With thy brush,
In thee the melody of the world had life.

As we went side by side,
Suddenly thou didst pause

And vanish in the darkness of night.
Since then I have gone forward, day and night,
Through so many joys and sorrows.
Across the ocean of the sky sweeps endlessly
The ebb and flow of light and darkness;
The pageant of flowers moves on in its glowing colours.
Through a thousand channels the restless stream of life
Pours to a cataract, defying death.
To the tune of the Unknown I keep step,
Going from the far to the far beyond;
The joy of the road has taken possession of me;
Where thou hast stepped aside from the road,
There thou art still waiting.
The grass, the dust, those stars and moons and suns,
Behind them thou dost stand hidden,
A picture, only a picture.

What madness is this of the poet?
Only a picture?
No, no, thou art not only a picture.
Who says thou art still, weeping thy silent tears,
Held fast in the lines of thy picture?
Then the glow of joy had ceased,
And the river stayed its current,
And the cloud had wiped away its golden writing.
If the shadow of thy shining hair
Played no longer on this earth,
Then the spring wind,
Sighing restless through the forest,
Would have lost its meaning.
Have I forgotten thee?
Thou hast taken thy place at the very root of my life,
Therefore I forget thee.

When I walk listlessly along the path,
Do I not forget the wayside flowers?
Do I not forget the stars?
And yet they sweeten the breath of life
And fill the void of forgetfulness with fair melody.
To be unconscious is not to forget;
Thou art no more before mine eyes,
Thou hast taken thy place within.
Thou art, therefore, the green within the green,
And the blue above the blue.
My world has found its harmony in thee.
We do not know that thy spirit speaks in my songs;
Thou art the poet within the heart of the poet.
Thou art no picture, no mere picture.
Long ago in the dawn I found thee,
Then I lost thee in the night.
And now in the darkness, hidden from all,
I am finding thee anew.
No picture, no mere picture art thou.

1. Tagore wrote this poem in memory of his wife.

TĀJ- MAHAL [1]

THIS you knew, O Emperor Shajahan,
That youth, glory and riches all pass away
In the stream of Time.
Might the sorrow of his heart
Be made deathless,
That was the desire of the Emperor.
Let the pomp of regal power
Vanish like the last glow of the sunset sky,
But may one deep sigh
Make tender the heavens,
This was your wish.
The lustre of all your diamonds and pearls
Is like the rainbow,
Spreading enchantment over the distant sky ;
If that lustre dims, let it vanish,
But may this *Tāj-Mahal* glisten bright
Like a tear drop on the cheek of Time.
Oh mind of Man,
You have no time to look backwards,
You hurry along the stream of life from port to port,
Taking up burdens at one
And laying them down at the other.
At the whisper of the south wind,
The spring flowers that fill the skirt of the forest,
Are scattered to dust
At the approach of twilight.
There is no time to linger.

Therefore in the wintry night the *Kunda*
Blossoms anew to adorn tearful autumn's tray of delight.
O Heart, you must leave all your gatherings by the wayside,
At the end of the day,
At the end of the night.
There is no time to linger and to look backward.
And so, Emperor, your anxious heart
Had desired to steal the heart of Time
Through Beauty's enchantment.
Flinging what garland round her neck,
Have you given to death that is formless,
A form immortal.
There is no time to mourn in the busy flow of the years,
Therefore you have prisoned your restless cry
With the silent net of stern marble.
The love-names you used to call your beloved
On moon-light nights in the privacy of your chamber,
Those whispering love-calls you have here left behind
In the ear of the Infinite.
The tearful tenderness of love has blossomed
In these quiet stones as the flowers of Beauty.
O Poet-Emperor, this dream-picture of your heart,
This new ' Cloud-Messenger ',[2]
Is soaring in songs and rhythms toward that Unseen,
Where your beloved has become one
With the glow of early dawn,
The tender sigh of the weary eventide,
The ethereal loveliness of the *Chameli* in the moonlight,
And the shoreless region beyond all words
Whence the hungering eye returns baffled
From its quest.
Your messenger of Beauty,
Eluding the watchman of Time,

Proclaims eternally : " I have not forgotten,
I have not forgotten, O beloved."

You have passed away, O Emperor.
Your empire has vanished like a dream
And your throne lies in the dust.
The memory of your warriors
Under whose tramp the earth once shuddered,
Is borne on the dust-laden winds of Delhi.
Your musicians sing no more,
The strains of the *nahabat* [3] mingle no more
With the ripples of the Jumna.
The jingling music of the princesses' anklets
Which died down amidst the forsaken ruins,
Reappears in the cry of the crickets
And resounds in the darkness of the night.
Still your messenger, untired and unfailing,
Ignoring the rise and fall of empires,
The rhythm of life and death,
Proclaims through the ages
With the voice of the eternal-bereaved :
" I have not forgotten, I have not forgotten,
O beloved."

It is a lie !
Who says that you have not forgotten ?
That you have not opened the doors of the cage of memory ?
Does your mind still cleave
To the twilight gloom of the past ?
Through the liberating path of forgetfulness
Has it not yet come out into the open ?
The shrine stands firm in the dust of the earth
And gently covers death with the veil of memory.

Who can keep life still ?
Every star of the sky beckons it on.
Its call vibrates from world to world
In the surging light of ever new dawns.
Breaking the bonds of remembrance,
It surges forth,
Free and unburdened,
Along the open road of the Universe.
Emperor,
No empire has ever been able to keep you in bondage ;
This sea-girt earth cannot satisfy you,
O Mighty One !
Therefore at the end of life's feast
You leave this earth behind,
Pushing it aside with your feet
Like an outworn earthen vessel.
You are mightier than your deeds,
Therefore the chariot of your life again and again
Leaves those deeds behind.
Therefore only traces of you remain,
But you yourself are not here.
⁴ That love which cannot urge one forward,
That love which sets its throne in the common highway,
The allurements of its sensuous pleasure
Cling round your feet like the dust of the wayside.
All that you have given back again to dust.
Into that dust where your footprint fell,
Suddenly unawares, wafted on the wings of air,
A seed dropped from the garland of life.
You have travelled far away,
But that seed, taking immortal life, raises itself to the sky
And chants in solemn melody :
" However far I look, he is not there, the traveller.

Not stopping to pick up or gather anything.
No sorrow, no trouble disturbs you.
In the joy of the road you spend all your earnings.

In the moment of fullness you possess nothing,
Therefore you remain ever pure.
At the touch of your feet,
The dust of earth becomes clean
And death shines forth as life.
If you stop for a moment,
Tired,
Then the universe would become choked with Matter,
Heaped sky-high ;
The lame, the dumb, the ugly, the deaf, the blind,
All gross Matter would gather and block the way.
The minutest atom would putrefy under its gathered weight,
And pierce the heart of the universe
With the dart of pain and poison.
O dancer. O celestial nymph. O unseen Beauty.
Your dance is like the flow of *Mandākini* [1]
Which ever renews and purifies the life of the universe
In the bath of death,
And the heavens blossom in perfect purity.

O Poet ! this sea-rounded earth,
Ringing with the playful, unceasing movements of invisible
     steps,
Has made your heart restless.
In each beat of your pulse I hear the footfall of the Restless.
Nobody knows that in your blood
Dance the waves of the ocean
And murmur the sighs of forests.
Today I remember
How I have noiselessly floated down the stream of Time,

Slipping from life to life,
Changing from form to form.
In the night, in the morning,
All I received, I gave away
In ever new gifts,
In ever new songs.

O hearken !
That stream has become resonant,
And the bark is heaving on its waves.
Leave behind
All you have gathered on the shore.
Let the voice of the future
Draw you out in one sweeping current—
From the clamour of the past
Into the fathomless darkness,
Into the limitless light.

1. The river that flows in heaven.

Note. This poem brings to mind the cosmic dance of Lord Shiva who dances the mystic dance, *Tāndava*, which creates and destroys the world in cycles. He is surrounded by a flaming aureole and tramples on the demon of evil. Shiva is also called *Rudra*, the Terrible One, and *Natarāja*, the King of dancers. He represents the transmutative and destructive aspects of the Godhead, while *Brahma* and *Vishnu* represent the creative and conservative aspects of the Hindu Trinity.

In this and several other poems recurs again and again, as a *leitmotif*, the idea that in possessions and in the static state lie the seeds of decay, whereas in giving away and in the dynamic movement of life and death, lies spiritual health. In the young, as opposed to the middle-aged and the old, the poet seems to find this ideal partly realized.

Like the *Dhyani-Buddha* (Buddha in meditation), *Shiva's Tandavanritya* (cosmic dance) has been immortalized in the supremest works of Indian sculpture, and a reader who has been fortunate enough to see one of these in reproduction, can better follow the imagery of these poems. Cf. 2, 3, 16, 18, 36, 37, 44, 45.

TĀJ-MAHAL (2)

Who gives you life, O Stone?
Who provides you,
Year by year, with the nectar of Immortality?
You hold up to the heavens eternally
This Joy-flower of earth,
And round you blows all the year
The sad breath of parting Spring.
The tear-dipped songs that died away
At the end of the night of union,
Lit by the dim candle, are still echoing
Ceaselessly in your heart,
O Stone, deathless Stone!

From his torn heart,
The bereaved Emperor brought out the jewel of
        separation
And laid it in the hand of the Universe,
For all to behold.
The royal guards are not there to keep watch;
All the heavens embrace her;
The sky imprints on her gently
One silent kiss of Eternity.
The first rays of the morning sun
Throw their crimson glow upon her,
And the pale rays of the moon,
With a sad smile of parting,
Make her tender!

O Empress ! through Beauty's enchantment
The memory of your love has become sublime.
That memory, incorporeal and ethereal,
Taking form,
Merges the Emperor's love with the Love universal,
And spreads beyond you to the whole world
In the imperishable light of life !
From the secrecy of the royal chamber
You have brought your glorious crown
And placed it on the heads of all lovers,
From dwellers in palaces to those in the meanest huts.
The memory of your love has sanctified them all.

The Emperor has taken leave of his own royal deed.
Today, the eternal sorrow of the mind of Man,
Embracing this marble Beauty,
Is seeking its realization night and morn !

O BELOVED,
This noon, what gift shall I bring thee?
A song of the early dawn?
Alas, the dawn fades away in the burning sun,
And my weary song is done.
O friend,
Coming to my door,
What dost thou want at the day's end,
And what shall I bring thee?
The evening lamp?
Its light is for the lonely corner,
The silent room,
And thou wilt carry it to where men gather.
Alas, it blows out in the wind.

What power have I to give thee a gift,
Flower or wreath, how canst thou stand the weight
When it withers in a day?
Whatever I put in thy hands
Will join with the dust,
Forgotten by the languid fingers,
And falling to the ground.
Rather,
When at thy leisure
Thou lingerest in my garden,
The perfume of an unseen flower,
Blown by a Spring breeze,
Shall startle thee.
That is my gift, unexpected, to thee.

Walking down my avenue,
Sleep shall come upon thine eyes,
And suddenly shalt thou see
From the locks of evening, a crimson ray descend
Gently across thy dreams.
That light is my unknown gift to thee.

In sudden flashes
My finest treasure comes,
And in a twinkling disappears.
Nameless it remains
Moving past as a melody,
Out of reach of hands, of voice.
Friend.
What thou wilt receive from there
Unasked,
 That will be truly thine.
Paltry and poor is what I myself give,
Fruit it may be, or song.

O Beautiful One !
When in mad revelry they pass by
Throwing dust at thee,
My heart cries out :
" O Emperor, pass thy judgment upon them ! "
Then, what do I see ?
The doors to thy Judgment Hall are wide open,
And thy Judgment is being given day and night.
The morning light bathes silently
Their blood-shot guilty eyes,
The perfume of flowers touches their rapacious breath,
And the light of the Seven Saints,[1]
Like temple-lamps lit by a worshipper,
Gaze steadily through the night upon their debauchery,
They who throw dust at thee !
O Beautiful One,
Thy Judgment is
In the fields of flowers,
In the pure air,
In the humming of insects,
In the warbling of the birds in Spring,
In the murmur of leaves by the wave-kissed shore !

O my Beloved,
They are relentlessly cruel,
Their appetites irresistible !
They lurk to steal thy ornaments
To decorate their naked passions.
When their blows fall upon Love

I can endure it no more,
In tears I cry out :
" Unsheathe thy sword, O my Beloved,
Execute thy Judgment ! "
Then ! What do I see ?
Mother's tears of forgiveness fall upon their rage,
The steadfast faith of the beloved
Takes their dart of pain
To her bleeding heart.
Beloved,
Thy Judgment dwells
In the silent ache of sleepless love,
In the stainless modesty of the pure wife,
In the bleeding heart of the friend,
In the lover's night of waiting,
In the tear-drenched morn of utter forgiveness !

My Terrible One,
They are greedy, blind with passion !
Stealthily they break into thy house
Stealing thy treasures !
Too heavy is the burden of those stolen goods
Crushing them relentlessly.
Then with tears I beseech thee :
" O Terrible One, forgive them."
Then, what do I see ?
Thy forgiveness descends as a hurricane !
In the fury of that tempest
Their stolen riches are scattered to the four winds,
And prostrate they lie !
O Terrible One,
Thy forgiveness is
In the lightning and thunder,

In the fiery writing of the setting-sun,
In the pouring of blood,
In the sudden clash of battle.

1. The constellation of Ursa Major.

DAY and night this thought is always in me—
You shall give, always give.
In joy and sorrow,
My hands I stretched out to you,
Thinking,
You shall give, always give.

You have given, always given—
At times, little by little,
At times, in a flood-tide of generosity.
I took and scattered all in wanton play
Amidst the dust.
Always, always have you given,
And your unceasing gift has filled to the brim
Earth's cup.

Today at last, I can bear no more
Their burden,
Nor the eternal supplication of a beggar's heart.
The more I receive,
The more I crave.
Free, O free me
From this crushing debt.

Me you will take, take,
When will this prayer be fulfilled?
Casting away this cup
Fashioned by my thirst,
Blowing out the light

Whose flame quivers with expectation,
Adorning your neck with my garland,
You shall take me away
At last,
From the burden of your gifts
Into the pure light of the Void.

WHY does the mad Spring-wind
Rush through the leafless forest
In these damp winter hours
Spreading, shameless and fearless
And with loud laughter,
Over the sky, unrest?

Brought by the hand of capricious Spring,
With a gesture of thoughtless song,
Here is a letter out of a youthful day
From one forgotten.

It says :
"For you I lie in the soft southwind,
For you in the breathing of Spring,
Awake to the noon day's pleasant flute,
And live, as does youth,
In eternal lands."

It says :
"Only I am always yours
Now and across the years,
Here and on other shores.
Come, at the end of life's worn path,
Leaving your withered wreath behind.
Come, and open the gate of death.
Dreams and hopes will resolve to a dust,
Flowers and high leaves fall,
While I, only I, shall remain."

14

Because of the " *Tapasya* " [1]
Of countless ages past,
This creeper has bloomed
On the lap of earth today.
This picture of joy lay hidden
In the folds of the Unknown.

Likewise in my dreams,
In the grove of a far-distant Spring
Shall bloom a smile
On the face of the dawn—
This hope slumbers
In the depth of my being.

1. Intense meditation, combined with austerities, undertaken to attain a spiritual goal.

My songs are like waterplants,
They do not stay immovable
Where they were born.
They have no roots,
Only flowers and leaves.
With the joy of light
They dance in the waves.
Having neither home nor wealth,
They are like unknown guests,
No one knows
When they come or go.

When the July rains come
Pouring down from the clouds
And submerge the banks,
My waterplants,
Turbulent and restless,
Lose their way in the flood,
And are carried away in all directions
From country to far country.

16

THE massive universe breaks out in laughter.
The dust, the sand,
Like children in rough, constant play
Dance eternally, dance in time.

The unnumbered, unseen thoughts and desires of man
At the call of Matter, mad with Form,
Grow drunk,
And long to join in their play.
Dreams, drifting and confounded,
Seek their shore.
Falling into the vague, bottomless flood,
These seek to hold fast to the earth
With grips of wood and iron,
Resting a moment there.
The relentless effort of the Mind congeals into Matter,
Becoming a city—
It is not mere brick and stone.

Whispering to the Void,
Those homeless, unheard voices of the past
Seek mine, where men gather.
Through shadows, those dark pilgrims march
To light.
Leaving the cavern of my mind,
All unbodied dreams race out
And thirsting for Form
They start to cross the dark desert.

How many shall take shape
In the ineffable light?
On that day shall be forgotten
Whence they spread their wings.
What poet unawares shall find them?
That palace still unseen,
From what sacred ground shall it arise?
And from what canon smoke
Shall come his triumphant call?

17

O World,
As long as I loved thee not,
So long thy light searched all its treasures
In vain.
So long the entire heaven,
Breathless by the wayside stood,
With lamp in hand.

My love came by, singing songs,
Whispering who knows what?
His garland he put round thy neck.
With a smile from enraptured eyes,
Unseen he gave thee
What shall remain eternally
In the hidden heart,
Woven in thy wreath of stars.

As long as I am stagnant,
I gather great wealth
And never sleep ;
Like an insect I gnaw the earth.
Heavier grows the weight of sorrow,
Life, with its cautious brain and chill of doubt
Grows white with age.

When I move,
Then in that Movement, beaten by Fate's blow,
My mask drops off,
And the gathering of pain dissolve.
Purified from that bath of Movement,
I come,
And drinking its ambrosia,
Youth blooms constantly new.

Therefore I am the eternal wayfarer,
Looking always forward.
Why vainly call me back?
I shall not, called by Death's secret love
Remain caged by the walls of my chamber.
With the garland of welcome in my hand
I shall greet ageless Youth.
Every burden shall I fling away—
The piled-up heaps of old age.
O Mind,
The infinite heavens are full
With the joyful song of the journey ;
Riding your chariot, the great Poet sings
With the stars, and the moon, and the sun.

I HAVE loved the world
And have wrapped it within my heart in numberless
    folds.
The light and shadow of night and morn
Have flooded my consciousness,
Till my life and my world have become one.
I have loved the light of the world,
Therefore I love this life.
Yet I know,
I shall have to take leave of it one day.
My voice will no more blossom in this air,
Nor my eyes bathe in this light.
My heart will not rush forth to greet the early dawn,
Nor will the starry night whisper her secrets
Into my ears.

One day,
I shall have to see her for the last time,
And whisper to her my parting words.
To long for her so ardently
Is as real as to have to renounce her
Utterly !
Between Life and Death
There must somewhere be a harmony ;
Otherwise the world
Could not have borne through the ages,
Smiling such a cruel deceit,
And all the lights of her stars
Would have darkened !

LET the strains of jubilant song
Play on my flute of pain,
And the loosed bark
Sway in the sea of tears.

The driving wind has risen, oh risen,
And the whole night through
No sleep has come.

To the wild laughter of the waters
Dances my heart;
O friend unknown, play out a tune
On my flute of pain.

O thou Unknown,
Play strange, new melodies
On my flute of pain,
And let my bark drift
In the rising wind.

In my heart rings the call from him
Whom I have never known;
So wonderfully am I called,
How can I stay at home?

The hope for a home has gone,
And in the blue abundance I have plunged.
You madcap,
Play out some strange melody,
On my flute of pain.

O YE, ye could not wait !
The Winter is not yet gone.
Hearing whose call
Have ye broken out in songs ?
O mad *Chāpa*,[1] O crazy *Bakul*,[1]
For whom have ye rushed out in eager wonder ?
Ye are the first who rush to death.
Ye do not pause to think
That your time has not yet come.
There is tumult in the branches,
Colour and scent blaze through the woodland.
Jostling each other in loud laughter,
Ye bud, Ye bloom ;
Ye drop, Ye fall.

Spring will arive in time.
Borne on the flood-tide of the south wind.
Ye did not wait to count the days
But straightaway piped your flutes !
What ye possessed,
Ye scattered along the path
In tears, in laughter.
O Ye mad, ye thriftless,
Hearing his footfall from afar,
Ye rushed into death
To cover the dust along the path.
Ye tarried not to see him with your eyes,
But all your fetters vanished
Before hearing, before seeing.

1. Name of Indian flowers.

WHEN to your side you called me caressingly,
I was afraid
Lest through carelessness I should lose you,
Lest going alone
I trample on the thorns of neglect.

But today
The hard strokes of neglect, beating humiliation's drum,
Bring out the music of freedom !
At last I have my release ;
The lock of pride lies shattered,
The fetters are loosened,
And the way lies open
To give and to take.

Heaven and Hell
Call me again with full might.
The storm that sweeps me away from home,
Has made me drunk with the wine of liberty.
Who can stop the humiliated ?
With the stars shooting down the night
Have I plunged through the yawning gulf,
Drawn by the pull of death.

I am that cloud of April
Driven hither and thither by violent storms ;
Casting away on the shores of the sunset
The golden crown,
The thunder-jewel it strung into its necklace,

I rush along the liberating path of neglect
To come with a humbled bow to your feet.

After birth, the babe feels his mother's love.
When he is wrapt in mother's womb
He knows her not.
When striking him,
You throw him from your protection,
Then through separation
Wakes awareness,
And he sees you.

1. In his essay *My Religion* the poet refers to this poem and develops the idea in detail. Not to make this note too long, I shall quote only a few passages.

" In the Old Testament it is said that man once dwelled in a Paradise where there was no sorrow, no death. But that heaven which I have not conquered through suffering, fighting against evil, is not a true heaven. Therefore, into this unconscious heaven came knowledge, and with it the conflict between truth and untruth, good and evil, life and death. When, transcending all these conflicts, man arrives again at the undivided truth, he errs no more. But where can all these conflicts be resolved ? In the heart of the Infinite. Therefore the *Upanishads* have said that *Brahma* is ' Truth, Knowledge, and Bliss '. When religious consciousness has awakened in man, he seeks reconciliation between sorrow and happiness, good and evil—he is then neither afraid of death nor eager to avoid suffering—his aim is directed towards the Absolute Good. But even this is not the final goal, which can only be love, bliss ! . . . The bliss that is awaiting him there is not the suppression of suffering but its supreme sublimation.

The path of religious awakening goes from life through death to immortality. . . . Therefore our prayer is : ' From untruth lead us into truth, from darkness into light, from death into life eternal.' "

At the beginning of Creation,
Out of the churning of the oceans,
Emerged two women—
The one, *Urbashi*, the peerless Beauty,
The nymph of heaven,
Queen in the realm of Desire ;
The other, *Lakshmi*, the Good,
The Mother of the World,
The Goddess enthroned in heaven.

The One, filling the cup
With the wine of fiery, boisterous Spring,
Steals the hearts of men,
Breaking their meditation,
And scatters them wild
Among the blossoming flowers
And songs of sleepless Youth.

The Other bathes his passion
In the cool dew of tears,
And brings him back to the peace or
Autumn's fullness,
To the benediction of the heavens,
To the temple of the Eternal,
Where mingle the rivers of
Life and Death.

O BROTHER,
Do you know where heaven is?
It has no beginning, it has no end,
Nor is it any country.

In virtue of good deeds performed in former
     lives,
I have at last been born
In the lap of Mother Earth.
Heaven therefore is fulfilled today
In my body,
In my loves and affections,
In the sighs of my heart,
In the joys and sufferings of my being.
She plays in ever new colours
On the wave of life and death.
In my heart
Heaven finds her home,
And in my songs
Her melodies.
She seeks me
In the joy that floods the sky.
Therefore the trumpet resounds
In the four corners of the earth
And echoes in the Seven Seas;
Therefore the flowers blossom
And there is joyous commotion
In waterfall and forest leaves.

Heaven has come to birth
In the lap of Mother Earth,
And in glad response
These tidings are lifted in the wind.

THE Spring that once came
To my courtyard
With its boisterous laughter,
And overwhelmed the forest leaves
With its passionate kiss,
Comes noiselessly today
To my lonely hut.
There in silence it tarries
At my threshold,
And with unwinking eyes
Gazes far into distance,
Where the green earth
Merges into the blue.

ON this Spring morning, along the sea-side way,
Leaves thrilled in blossom,
As if they flowered out of my own heart's vine
Like blood-red pain.
From time to time
They swayed in the south wind,
And rustling murmurs rose in the sky ;
My days passed away in humming songs.

When the Spring shall come again,
Spreading its coloured sail in the south wind,
Setting all on fire,
My golden flowers of love shall bloom
In my heart's vine,
And the bliss of my heart
Dance to the tune of my songs.

My King remains unknown to me,
So when he calls me to pay my rent,
I want to run, deceive,
And leave my debts unpaid.
Wherever I may hide myself,
His summons is always there,
In every breath,
Behind my work,
In my dreams and in my nights.

Thus do I realize
That he knows me well.
I know now,
By selling my house
I cannot even my account with him.
Therefore I have decided,
That all I possess in life and death,
I will offer at his feet.
And then,
Through my own efforts
And in my own right,
I shall find home
In his dominion.

To the bird you have given song,
Therefore it sings ;
To me you have given only a voice,
But I give back more—
I sing.

The wind you have made free,
Therefore it lightly obeys your commands ;
But me you have loaded with burdens,
With them I toil on.
Passing from death to death,
Slowly I free myself from them,
Till empty-handed I come
Ready to serve you.

The full-moon, you have endowed with a smile,
It pours forth its loveliness
And fills with beauty the cup of earth.
My brow which you have touched with sorrow,
I wash with tears, transforming it into joy.
Mingling darkness with light
Have you created your earth ;
To that earth you send me
Empty-handed.
Watching me with a smile hidden behind your void,
You command me to transform it into heaven.
To all you give,
Only from me do you demand.
Descending from your throne,

Smilingly you take to your heart
What out of love I offer you.
What you lay in my hands,
A thousand times enriched
It returns to you.

WHEN you were alone, you did not know yourself;
There was then no waiting by the wayside,
And the winds charged with tears
Did not blow from this bank to the other.
I came and your sleep vanished,
And flowers of joy blossomed everywhere.
You made me bloom in countless flowers
And rocked me in a cradle of many forms.
Scattering me amidst the countless stars
You gathered me up again in your lap.
Hiding me behind the curtain of death
You find me ever anew.

I came,
And your heart trembled.
I came,
And with it came your sorrows
And your fiery joy
And ardent spring,
Raising storms of life and death.
I came,
And therefore you came too.
Seeing me,
And touching me,
You felt your own touch.
In my eyes is shame
And in my heart fear,
And a veil covers my face.
I tremble to look at you.

Yet I know, O Lord,
You are longing to meet me ;
Otherwise all suns and stars
Were created in vain.

Note. There is a very ancient religious fraternity in Bengal—the *Baul* Singers—who, with a one-stringed harp, go from village to village, singing songs of love to God. To them, as to the mystic poets of mediaeval India, God manifests Himself as Love. They call Him, " *Maner-Manush* ", which means, " Man of my Heart ". They adore Him as lover and friend. The *Baul* Singers are simple rustics, often unlettered. They do not follow any rituals, but their hearts are filled with the all-pervading presence of God. They sing :

" Ah, where am I to find Him, the Man of my Heart ?
Alas, since I lost Him, I wander in search of Him,
Through lands near and far.

" Love is my golden touch—it turns desire into service ;
Earth seeks to become Heaven, man to become God.

" As we look on every creature, we find each to be His incarnation.
What can you teach us of His ways ? In ever-new play He wondrously revels."

Chandidas, a Bengali mediaeval poet, sings :

" How could the Scripture know the meaning of the Lord who has His play in the world of human forms ?
Listen, O brother man, the truth of man is the highest truth, there is no other truth above it."

Kabir, the weaver, sings :

" I would not go, my heart, to Mecca or Medina,
For behold, I ever abide by the side of my Friend.
Mad would I become, had I dwelt afar, not knowing Him.
There's no worship in Mosque or Temple ; or special holy day.
At every step I have my Mecca and Kashi [1] ; sacred is every moment."

[1] Kashi is another name for Benares, the holiest pilgrimage for Hindus.

(*Continued at foot of page 55*)

On this tiny raft
I shall cross the river of life.
When twilight descends,
I shall discard and heed it no more.
Let it drift away.
Then what shadows, what lights !

I am a pilgrim of the Unknown—
That is my joy.
It raises and resolves
All my conflicts.
No sooner has the Known bound me fast in her net,
Than appears the Unknown
And it bewilders me !

The Unknown is my helmsman,
My deliverance !
With him is my covenant.
His love is terrible,
With his terror he breaks my fear,
He heeds not the caution of the old.
Breaking the shell,
He frees the pearl.

Perhaps you brood and ask if the past returns,
And the raft pulls alongside the old pier.
No, it will not.
You are afraid of what lies ahead.
Are you so poor
That only the past is you ?
All fetters shall break, shall tear.

O poet ! The hour has struck ;
End thy banquet.
The waves flow in the flood-tide.
He has not yet shown his face,
Therefore my heart throbs.
In what form shall the Unknown come to me ?
In what new colours, at the shore of what sea ?

Tagore was very much attracted to their songs, and many of his own songs echo the same sentiments.

Those who are interested in this subject should read Tagore's, *The Religion of Man* (publ. 1931), from which the quotations are taken.   Cf. 5, 12, 17, 20, 24, 28, 29, 30, 31, 32, 33, 34, 40.

With all its riches,
Your universe lies at your feet.
There is no want.
In yourself, you are complete.
Yet all your riches and honour bring you no joy.
You shall make your treasure my own,
And thus shall they become ever new to you.
You buy anew your sunrise through my eyes.
Thus you come to know
The touchstone of your love,
Turning my heart into gold.

THE sunset sky put a jewel in her glistening hair
At the end of the day ;
I thread it on my stringless necklace
Hidden within me.
Over the still *Padma* shores flying,
The evening touched my face—
Touched me with flowers
I brought to your feet—
And floated on the still waters
Such a fleet of stars,
And spread on the face of the night
Her golden cloth.
Riding its black steed
Along the shadowy path of the Seven Saints,[1]
She raised dust of fire
And took her leave.
In one poet,
She left on his forehead a touch
Tender in its infinity.
Such an evening has never been,
Nor will it ever be again.
Thus, O Lord,
Into the fragile moment's cup
Pouring the fairest heavenly wine,
You make it freshly new.

1. The constellation of Ursa Major.

My footsteps
I know you hear night and day.
Your pleasure
Blooms in the purple of Autumn's dawn,
Sparkles in the springtime shower of blossoms.
The nearer I come to you on your path,
The livelier dances the sea.
Like lotus-petals my life unfolds
From birth to birth,
And your crowding suns and stars
Circle me in wonder.
The blossom of the world woven of light
Fills your offering hands,
And your shy heaven
Unfolds its love,
Petal by petal,
In my sky.

TODAY,
The window of my mind opens suddenly towards you,
And I, remaining and gazing still,
Bathed in the morning light,
Forget my work.
The name with which you always call me,
Echoed in the trembling of the April leaves.
Therefore I remain, and gazing still
Now in the morning light,
Forget my work.

In the morning light
Through your universe
I breathe out songs,
Echoes of your own.
These I learn, sitting at your feet.
Therefore I remain, and gazing still
Now in the morning light,
Forget my work.

WHEN dew falls as tears from the morning sky,
When riverside trees sparkle in sunlight,
So close in my heart their shadows fall,
Then I know
The Universe is a floating lotus
In the holy lake of my mind.[1]
Then I know
I am the voice within the Voice,
The song within the Song,
The life within the Life,
The light breaking through the heart of Darkness.

1. *Manoswara* in the original. It is also the name of a lake in Tibet and is of great sanctity. In high summer, every year, thousands of pious Hindus make a pilgrimage to this holy lake. In mythology it is the legendary source of the four world rivers (actually the rivers Oxus, Indus, Ganges, and Brahmaputra rise from sources not too far distant from this holy lake) which water the four great continents—the four petals of the World Lotus.

O THE YOUTHFUL, the Unripe,
The Evergreen, the Foolish,
Breathe life into the half-dead !
Drunk with the blood-red light of the morn,
Let them say what they will.
Making light all their arguments
Dance with thy spirits high !
Come ! O Unruly, the Evergreen !

A parrot's cage sways mildly in the air.
Lo ! there the Judicious and Overripe
Covers its eyes and ears with wings,
And in the gloom of its locked-up cage
Drowses and is still as in a picture !
Come ! O Living, the Evergreen !

Nobody looks into the distance,
Nobody sees the flood has come
And the waves toss high.
They do not want to walk on this earth,
They sit firm, spreading their mats on the floor.
Come ! O Restless, the Evergreen !

Everyone shall caution thee:
When they see the sudden light flash upon them,
They cry out : " Why this disturbance ? "
Under the clash of arms they shall wake,
Leaving their beds rush forth,

And between Right and Wrong
Begin the battle.
Come ! O Headstrong, the Evergreen !

The altar of the Goddess of Fetters—
Shall it remain ever-standing ?
O the Furious ! break open the door.
Tearing asunder the skies with thy boisterous laughter,
Waving high the banner of Victory,
Empty the purse,
And bring out thy choicest failures.
Come ! O Intoxicated, the Evergreen !

Leave behind the highway,
Become a homeless wanderer,
And blaze a trail into the Unknown.
Danger lies ahead,
Let Sorrow be thy companion.
Knowing this my heart dances !
Stop seeking precepts in age-grey manuscripts.
Come ! O Liberated, the Evergreen !

Casting off
All that is weak, infirm and worn,
Scatter life in an endless stream.
With the intoxication of the Green
Thou hast made the earth brim,
And thy light flashes in the crumbling cloud !
Throw round the neck of Spring thy own garland.
Come ! O Deathless, the Evergreen !

Do you hear the tumult of death afar,
You who are poverty-stricken and indifferent?
The cries and the waves of blood pouring from a million hearts?
Amid the fire-floods and poisonous storm-clouds
Comes the call of the captain,
To steer the ship to an unknown shore.
For the time is over—the time of waiting in the port—
When goods are bought and sold in an endless round.
Dishonesty mounts up high and the well of Truth runs dry.
Therefore one hears the call of the captain:
"Steer the ship through storm to a new shore."
The sailors rush forth from their huts with oars in their hands.

They wake up in sudden fear and ask:
"When will the golden portals of the dawn open?"
The gathered clouds of storm have darkened the sky.
And no man knows if the night is past.
The waves toss high on the horizon.
And amidst their roar is heard the captain's voice:
"Forward, forward, to the new shore."
Who have rushed out? The beds of ease are emptied.
The mother cries and the beloved stands silently by the door.
Above the thunder and the storm, rises the wail of parting.
"Sail forth, O Sailors," comes the command,
"For the time in the harbour is over."

Piercing death, the ship sails forth tossed by the waves.
No time to ask to which port she steers, or when she arrives.
Only this the sailors know,

That living or dying,
Battling with the waves,
With sails full spread and helm held firm,
They must hold on for the new shore.
Unknown is that shore, unknown that country.
In the voice of the storm the call of that unknown shore
Resounds from end to end.
Through the thick darkness,
On the way to the New Life rings the song of Death.
In the impenetrable night,
All the sorrows of the world,
All its sins and evils,
Its tears and cruelties,
Have risen in tumult, overflowing their banks
And blaspheming the skies.
Yet, O fearless, O sorrow-stricken one,
With the groanings of the earth resounding in your ears,
Accept the mad evil days with fortitude,
And with hope undimned in your soul,
Hold on for the new shore.
O Brother, whom do you blame?
Bow down your head.
It is your sin and mine.
The ulcer grows in the heart of God for ages—
The cowardice of the weak,
The arrogance of the strong,
The cruel greed of the greedy,
The rancour of the wronged,
The pride of race, and the insult to the divinity in Man—
These have burst at last,
And scour earth and sea with the breath of destruction.
Let the tempest rage and the wind rise,
And all the thunders of the world exhaust themselves.

Stop your evil tongue and curb your pride of righteousness.
With your mind intent, cross this sea of chaos,
And sail to that shore of new creation !

Sorrow have I found every day,
Evil have I met in many guises ;
The whirlpool of restlessness troubles the stream of life,
And death plays hide and seek, embracing the whole world.
They all pass away, mocking the world with their transient
    laughter.
To-day they have piled themselves heaven-high.
Face them with an unflinching heart, and say :
" I do not fear you, O Monster,
For I have conquered you every hour of my life !
I am more real than you—with this faith will I die.
Peace is real, the Good is real,
And real is the Eternal One."

If the deathless dwell not in the heart of death,
If truth is not gained in fight with sorrow,
If sin dies not in the shame of its own revealment,
If pride breaks not under the intolerable burden of its pomp,
Then whence comes the hope that drives these men from their
    homes
Like stars rushing to their deaths in the morning light ?
Shall the value of heroes' blood and mothers' tears
Be utterly lost in the dust of the earth ?
Shall it not win heaven ?
Shall not the world's Treasurer repay this debt ?
The travail of the night, will it not usher in the dawn ?
In the night of sorrow, under death's blow,
When Man bursts his mortal bounds,
Will not God stand revealed
In His Glory ?

THIS yearning of my body—
What does it want to say?
Into my heart has come the new and the fresh,
Therefore I have put on this new veil.
It is like the wave of the new flooding my body,
It is bordered with song to draw around my breast.

I have given myself to him,
Yet ever anew offer this gift.
In my eyes sparkles new light,
Blooms a smile;
And with it my new veil
Brings my body afresh to him.

The light of the moon shall shine on the forest's shadow
Through the tearful songs of my eyes.
Then we two,
As the folds of my new veil whisper
Each to the other,
Shall meet in the midst of the Universe.

Oh, my heart is like an evening sky,
The wild riot of colours does not cloy.
Therefore I change my many veils,
From colour to colour.
Look,
Today my veil is blue like rain-washed sky.

The hue of the sky is bewildering blue,
Merging with the forest's shade.
Today over my body blows the seaward wind,
And the new veil brings me
The message of the rain-drenched sky.

TO WILLIAM SHAKESPEARE [1]

O UNIVERSAL POET,
Whose sun rose on a distant shore,
England found you in her breast,
Thought you were her own,
Kept you—
Kissing your shining brow—
In forest boughs a while embraced,
In dew-bright dales removed,
Where fairies danced and flowers bloomed.
Not yet did the island groves resound
With singing praise for this rising sun.
Then, he leaped the horizon's lap
Wordlessly called from Infinity,
Climbed in the centuries hour by hour,
To reach the zenith of his glory,
Enlightening the mind of a world.

See now,
From far *Bhārat's* [2] shore,
From her cocoanut groves,
At this end of an age,
Rings his song of victory.

1. At the request of the Shakespeare Society this poem was written on the three-hundredth death-anniversary of the great Poet.
2. Ancient name for India.

You, who look out through the window of my eyes
Into this morning light,
Your vision brings floating to my mind
The infinite song of the skies,
The generous touch of silence !
I feel today,
As if from the distant shore of my memory
You have seen so many vistas,
In countless worlds and ages,
In solitude and amidst the crowd.

All that you have seen vibrates today
In the tremor of the grasses,
In the whispering of the forest leaves.
Under how many veils
You have secretly glimpsed the face of the one Beloved,
In countless forms,
Through innumerable births,
In the twilight of nameless worlds !

Therefore in the infinite sky,
The song of your primaeval union,
And your eternal parting, resounds
In one perfect pain.
Therefore what you see
Is encompassed by what you do not see.
Therefore the south wind,
Heavy with the scent of flowers,
Is surcharged with infinite yearning
And the eye-to-eye and ear-to-ear love-whisperings
Of countless births !

ALL this I long to say but it remains unuttered :
The world has always shewn my eyes its myriad images ;
I do not find words simple enough to express
How these glimpses of the Unknown have filled my heart
With joy profound !

The song of the lonely plains echoes
Under the shadow of the solitary *Banyan* ;
The peasant ploughs the fields by the gentle slope of the river,
Over those treeless, desolate banks the swan flies past,
The tired, dried-up river drowses leisurely like one half asleep,
The ageless path curves its way along the rice field like a friend,
And binds in fellowship river and hut.

This village and those fields,
This landing-place and the faint blue trace of the river
All bathed in winter light,
The noisy meeting of waterfowls on the solitary banks—
How often have not these sights greeted the Poet ?
Just to sit and gaze,
To drift with the stream,
This light and this breeze,
The hum of sounds half audible,
The shadows cast on the river from clouds
Floating aimlessly—
All these joys and yearnings,
That again and again have made life forlorn,
Seek their utterance today.

You I have humiliated, again and again.
You came in the morning with a song;
Because you disturbed my sleep, I threw stones at you.
Next moment you were lost in the crowd.
Like a beggar you came to my door,
But I turned you away.

In the evening you came torch in hand,
Dim and strange like an evil dream.
Taking you to be an enemy,
I barred all my doors.
A shiver ran through the darkness.
For this you came, my unknown friend,
So that I might refuse you,
Turn you back,
Strike you.

Then at the dead of night,
When the lamp goes out,
I shall feel lonely without him
Whom I turned away.
In this life,
Those whom I have welcomed with great honour and
    eagerness
Will vanish and merge into darkness.
He I ignored,
Did not know,
Did not understand—
His face shall appear again before my sleepless eyes

In the light of the stars.
In the perfume of the *Rajanigandha* [1] ;
His many departures shall echo in my heart
As many returns.

1. A flower that blossoms only at night.   Literally translated, the name
means : night-perfume.

WHY do you plague yourself with worries?
The play of joy and suffering,
Must it lie heavy on your heart
Like a crushing rock?
In whose chariot do you rush down the road?
Through aeons and aeons He will hold taut the reins.

As a baby you came to your mother's lap—
That day is gone.
Then in tears and laughter you spent
The mad swing of youth.
When at night, the lamp was lit,
Where was the present hour?
Again, what new melodies will resound
At the end of the day?

They are burdenless, who travel the road;
They have neither pots nor purses,
Homes nor property.
Their bodies are drifting clouds,
Their minds like whirlwinds in the air.

O traveller,
Strike up a marching melody,
And play upon your harp.
Shoreless is the wide sea—
May this glad tiding make your heart dance with joy.
Let each step along the way bring forth

Flowers of tears and laughter.
For you, the unbound,
Are the free south wind in Spring.

Let me end
This birth, this play of forms.
The day ends and twilight falls.
Let me put on my new robes.
At the time of parting, let me look back
And scatter my tears a little.

In that unknown land
The vision of the bride waits graciously.
The waves of my heart so dance and love !
In that distant realm
The flutes of light shall play a melody,
And in what new face shall that unknown flower
Blossom in smiles ?

One dew-wet morn, here, I unfolded my life,
And practised my songs on a harp.
This harp of my life's entirety,
I know, I must leave behind.
But their airs, filling my heart,
I shall take with me.

She to whom I shall sing these songs
At the edge of the new light's shore,
Is ever with me containing my world.
In Autumn,
Veiled she strides along the *Shiuli*-scented forest,
And in Spring,
She puts her garland round my neck.

Suddenly at the turn of the path she appears,
Lonely and forlorn,
Sitting at evening in the melancholy plain.
So she comes and goes,
And so, rustling the leaves,
The pain-charged wind through the mind's forest blows.

In the endless turn of ebb and tide, she comes and goes ;
Half in smiles, half in tears,
We come to know each other.
With her I could never build a home,
But strove for her on the open road,
Weaving with strings of coming and going,
Weaving a net of love.

O Youth !
Must you remain imprisoned in the cage of Happiness ?
You are the pilgrim of the pathless shore.
Your wings are restless and untiring,
And your flight
Soaring in search of your unknown nest,
Steals from the tempest its thunder !

O Youth !
Are you a mendicant beseeching Age ?
You are the hunter in death's dark forest.
In her cup
Death always keeps for you her nectar,
And your proud Beloved waits for you,
A veil of death concealing her face ;
Lift it and see her high loveliness.

O Youth !
What melodies are you practising ?
Your message,
Playing on the strings of the south wind
Brings to the forest awareness,
Rings in the death-dealing clouds of the tempest,
And rides in triumph on the waves.

O Youth !
Shall you remain imprisoned within your narrow circle ?
You have to tear Age's net of fascination.
May your flame, sharp as a dagger,

Pierce the mist of infirmity ;
And your immortal flower,
Unfolding in world after world,
Blossoms towards light !

O Youth !
Will you be prostrate in the dust
Buried beneath a burden of waste ?
For you brings dawn the crown of gold,
Fire shoots heavenwards,
And in you the sun sees his image.

THE BLESSING OF THE NEW YEAR [1]

THE last, tired night of the year has just passed away,
O wanderer !
On your path resounds the call of the burning sun,
Echoes the song of the Terrible One.[2]

O wanderer !
Let the dust of the open road be as your mother's lap.
Let the whirlwind of Movement
Taking hold of you,
Free you from the trammels of the earth
And leads you to the ends of the world !
Not for you is the welcome call of the conch-shell,[3]
Nor the lamp of evening,
Nor the tears of the beloved.
For you there waits by the wayside
The blessings of scorching April
And the thunder of rainy July.
At every corner lurks the bite of the roused serpent
And the greetings of thorns.
The abuse of the evil-tongued
Shall be your song of triumph—
Such is the gift of the Terrible One !

Losing all,
You will gain the priceless gift
Not visible to the eye.
You claimed Immortality—
That is neither pleasure nor comfort,

Neither peace nor rest !
From door to door you will be turned away,
Death shall wound you mortally—
Such is the blessing of the New Year,
Such the gift of the Terrible One !
Be fearless O wanderer !
The homeless Goddess of Illuck
Shall be the dispenser of all your blessings.

The last tired night of the year has just passed away,
O wanderer !
The Cruel One has appeared before your doors !
Let the bolts be removed
And the wine-glass shattered to pieces !
Hold fast to him
Whom you know not, nor comprehend.
Let his luminous message resound
In the beatings of your heart.
O wanderer,
The night has passed away ;
Let it pass,
The last night of the dying year.

1. The Bengali New Year is in April, the hottest month of the year.
2. In Bengali " Rudra ", another name for Lord Shiva. Between
cosmic periods Shiva dances the mystic dance (*Tāndava*) creating and
destroying the world.
3. Hindu households women blow the conch-shell on auspicious
occasions, such as birth, marriage, or to welcome an honoured guest.

ON the shores of *Bhārat*,[2]
Where men of all races have come together,
Awake, O my Mind !
Standing here with outstretched arms,
I send my salutations to the God of Humanity,
And in solemn chant sing His praises.
At whose call no one knows,
Came floating streams of men
And merged into the sea of *Bhārat*.
The Aryan, the Non-Ayran, the Dravidian,
The Huns, the Pathans and the Moghuls—
They all have merged here into one body.
Today the West has opened its doors,
And from thence come gifts.
Giving and taking,
All will be welcome on the shores of *Bhārat*,
Where men of all races have come together.

In mad exultation, singing songs of victory,
Have they come, crossing deserts and mountains ;
They all dwell within me
And in my blood echo their varied melodies.
O Terrible One !
Let the heavens resound with your music ;
Even those, whom in disdain we kept apart,
Will gather round thee, O *Bhārat*,
Where men of all races have come together.

Here one day in the hearts of men
The message of the One resounded.
In the fire of " *Tapasya* " [3] all differences were
    forgotten,
And the many forged into one.
Round that fire of sacrifice,
We all have to meet with bowed heads
And unite,
On the shores of *Bhārat*,
Where men of all races have come together.

In that fire,
The blood-shot flame of suffering is aglow.
O mind, bear this suffering
And hear the call of the One.
Conquer all shame, all fear,
And let vanish all humiliations.
What great life will emerge
At the end of the days of suffering.
The night ends,
The great Mother is awake
On the shores of *Bhārat*,
Where men of all races have come together.

Come, O Aryan and Non-Aryan,
Hindu and Muslim,
Come, O English and you Christian,
Come, O Brahmin,
Purify your mind and clasp the hands of all ;
Come, O downtrodden,
And let vanish all burdens of your humiliation.
Tarry not, but come you all

To anoint the Mother,
On the shores of *Bhārat*,
Where men of all races have come together.

1. This poem is taken from the Bengali edition of *Gitanjali* (publ. 1911).
2. *Bhārat* is the ancient name for India.
3. Intense concentration of mind in meditation.